# TEENAGE MUTANT NINJA TURTLES
## CHANGE IS CONSTANT · VOL. 1

Special thanks to Joan Hilty, Linda Lee, and Kat van Dam for their invaluable assistance.

ISBN: 978-1-63140-025-4

17 16 15 14        1 2 3 4

**IDW**®
www.IDWPUBLISHING.com
IDW founded by Ted Adams, Alex Garner, Kris Oprisko, and Robbie Robbins

Ted Adams, CEO & Publisher
Greg Goldstein, President & COO
Robbie Robbins, EVP/Sr. Graphic Artist
Chris Ryall, Chief Creative Officer/Editor-in-Chief
Matthew Ruzicka, CPA, Chief Financial Officer
Alan Payne, VP of Sales
Dirk Wood, VP of Marketing
Lorelei Bunjes, VP of Digital Services
Jeff Webber, VP of Digital Publishing & Business Development

Facebook: facebook.com/idwpublishing
Twitter: @idwpublishing
YouTube: youtube.com/idwpublishing
Instagram: instagram.com/idwpublishing
deviantART: idwpublishing.deviantart.com
Pinterest: pinterest.com/idwpublishing/idw-staff-faves

Story by **Kevin Eastman & Tom Waltz** · Script by **Tom Waltz** · Layouts by **Kevin Eastman** · Art by **Dan Duncan**
Colors by **Ronda Pattison** · Letters by **Robbie Robbins** · Series Edits by **Scott Dunbier & Bobby Curnow**

Cover by **Dave Wilkins** · Collection Edits **Justin Eisinger & Alonzo Simon**
Collection Design **Robbie Robbins** · Pages 1, 2, 3 art by **Dan Duncan**, Colors by **Ronda Pattison**
Page 4 art by **Kevin Eastman** · Colors by **Ronda Pattison**

OUR INDIVIDUAL TECHNIQUES ARE AS UNIQUE AS EACH NEW CRASH OF THUNDER.

GET IN THERE! I WANT THAT STINKIN' RAT AND THOSE SLIMY REPTILES DEAD!

BO STAFF?

COLDLY ANALYTICAL AND DELIBERATE.

BOW TIE!

GLKK.

MILITANTLY DISCIPLINED AND PRECISE.

WHOULF!

HYAA!

SORRY...

ABSURDLY UNORTHODOX AND CAREFREE.

OHHH...

...NO BABY GANGSTAS FOR YOU, DUDE!

IDIOTS!

GUESS IF I WANT SOMETHIN' DONE *RIGHT*...

WRETCHEDLY MISGUIDED AND VENGEFUL.

...I GOTTA DO IT *MYSELF!*

AND WITH THE BITTERSWEET EXPERIENCE OF CENTURIES.

I'M GONNA *TEAR* YOU APART!

I HAVE *DEFEATED* OLD HOB BEFORE.

GLGK!

THEN, AS NOW, THE BATTLE WAS FIERCE.

BUT WHAT ONCE WAS SOLELY A FIGHT FOR SURVIVAL...

...HAS BECOME VERY PERSONAL.

KEEP *PRESSING,* GUYS!

NO, OLD HOB...

...NOT *TODAY.*

YOU THINK THEY *GOT THE* MESSAGE?

YEP. IT'LL STILL BE *RINGING* LOUD AND CLEAR IN THEIR EARS TOMORROW.

THEN, WE CAN *ONLY* HOPE...

...THAT THEY *HEED* THE SOUND.

YOU'RE *DEAD!*

AHK!

EVENTUALLY, THE TEMPEST SUBSIDES.

YOU... I'LL GUT YOU *YET*, RAT. YOU'LL SEE... *ALL* OF YOU.

JUST LIKE THAT *OTHER STINKIN'* FREAK, YOU'RE ALL GONNA DISAPPEAR...

...AND BE *FORGOTTEN* FOREVER!

C'MON, GUYS, LET'S—

NO, WE ARE *DONE* HERE, MY SONS. WE MUST GO.

"...WE HAVE NOT FORGOTTEN."

IT IS SIMPLY THE CALM BEFORE THE NEXT STORM.

...ENDS IN UNCERTAIN SILENCE.

AND WHAT BEGAN WITH A FEROCIOUS ROAR...

RAPHAEL...

OH, DON'T WORRY ABOUT HIM. HE'S A PART OF ANOTHER, UM... SPECIAL PROJECT. HE'S ALWAYS RUNNING AROUND THE PLACE.

FREE?!

YEAH, W-WE HAVE A HARD TIME KEEPING HIM... CONTAINED. BUT, LIKE I S-SAID, HE'S HARMLESS.

IF YOU SAY SO. JUST PLEASE DON'T TELL ME HE'S PART OF SOME RAT SOUP PROGRAM OR I'M GONNA HURL.

HEH. RAT SOUP.

COME ON, WE SH-SHOULD GET YOU TO HUMAN RESOURCES. THEY SHOULD, UM... HAVE YOUR NEW INTERN BADGE READY TO PICK UP.

AND THEN I GUESS I'LL BE OFFICIAL, HUH, CHET?

YEAH...

...W-WELCOME TO STOCKGEN RESEARCH, MISS O'NEIL.

JUST *APRIL* IS FINE, CHET. THANKS.

...I WANT *YOU* TO TELL ME HOW MUCH BLASTED LONGER I'M GOING TO HAVE TO WAIT TO GET WHAT I'M PAYING YOU ALL THIS MONEY FOR.

GENERAL KRANG, I PROMISE YOU...

...WE WILL HAVE EVERYTHING YOU'VE ACQUISITIONED FROM US COMPLETED IN SHORT ORDER.

INCLUDING THE *MUTAGEN?*

YES, GENERAL, INCLUDING THE SUPER-SOLDIER MUTAGEN. AND I WILL DELIVER THEM ALL TO YOU *PERSONALLY* JUST AS SOON AS THEY ARE READY.

SEE THAT YOU *DO*, STOCKMAN. I'VE GOT A WAR TO FIGHT, AND I WILL *NOT* ACCEPT ANY MORE DELAYS.

AGAIN, MY APOLOGIES FOR OUR TARDINESS, BUT WHEN ALL IS SAID AND DONE, GENERAL KRANG, I'M CONFIDENT YOU WILL FIND THE WAIT WAS WORTHWHILE—

—VERY WORTHWHILE INDEED.

THREE MONTHS LATER.

YOU REALLY HAVE TAKEN TO THOSE *TURTLES*, APRIL...

...I'M EXPECTING YOU TO STEAL THEM AND TAKE THEM HOME ANY DAY NOW.

HA! I WISH I COULD, LINDSEY—THEY'RE JUST SO DARN PRECIOUS.

THE RAT, THOUGH? NOT SO MUCH.

SPLINTER? HE'S NOT SO BAD ONCE YOU GET TO KNOW HIM.

WHY DO YOU GUYS CALL HIM SPLINTER, ANYWAY?

OH, WELL, HE'S PART OF A PSYCHOTROPIC DRUG TEST WE'RE RUNNING. THE DRUG'S EFFECT IS LIKE SPLITTING—OR *SPLINTERING*—THE ANIMAL'S NATURE IN TWO.

BASICALLY, SEPARATING OUT A CAPACITY FOR HUMAN-LIKE *COGNITION* FROM THE INSTINCTUAL ANIMAL STATE. IN *THEORY*, AT LEAST.

PSYCHOTROPIC *DRUG TEST?* WHAT THE HECK DOES *THAT* HAVE TO DO WITH BIO-ENGINEERING MEAT?

LINDSEY?

UH, I JUST REMEMBERED, I'M SUPPOSED TO BE IN A TECHNICAL UPDATE MEETING RIGHT NOW. I... UH... I'LL SEE YOU GUYS LATER.

WELL, THAT WASN'T *TOO* WEIRD.

Y-YEAH, UM... YOU KNOW HOW THOSE TECHY TYPES CAN BE.

UH, CHET, *WE'RE* TECHY TYPES.

UM... HEH... YEAH.

SO, UM... APRIL. Y-YOU SHOULD GIVE THESE GUYS NAMES, TOO. YOU'RE AROUND THEM SO MUCH.

ACTUALLY, I ALREADY HAVE.

RE-REALLY? WHAT ARE THEY?

OKAY, LET'S SEE. THE LITTLE GUY STANDING ALL STILL AND QUIET IS *LEONARDO.*

THE ONE STUDYING THAT BUG IS *DONATELLO.*

AND THE ONE GORGING HIMSELF ON LETTUCE IS *MICHELANGELO.*

UH... I HAVE HISTORY OF RENAISSANCE ART 101 THIS SEMESTER.

UM... OKAY.

SO, WH-WHAT ABOUT THAT GUY?

OH, THE FEISTY ONE?

THAT'S *RAPHAEL.*

PRESENT DAY.

C'MON, C'MON...

...BINGO!

DINNER IS SERVED.

OH, NOW THAT'S JUST WRONG.

CRASH

WHAT THE...?

CHAPTER 2

PUT THE KID DOWN...

...NOW.

NGK!

URF!

HOW'S MY KNEE TASTE, HUH?

HKK!

I GREW UP ON THESE STREETS, PUNK... FIGHTIN' IS PART OF LIVIN'!

...LET ME SHOW YOU!

YAGH!

THUNK

FRIGGIN' NO GOOD, SONUVA...

AIN'T DONE YET? GOOD. 'CAUSE I CAN GO ALL NIGHT.

SCREW... SCREW YOU, MAN.

SCREW THE BOTH OF YOUSE!

RRRRRRRR

"...WHERE THE HECK DID YOU COME FROM?"

AHH!

FIFTEEN MONTHS EARLIER.

...YOU NEARLY GAVE ME A HEART ATTACK. *AGAIN!*

HUGE SCHOOL REPORT DUE IN THE MORNING AND *YOU* AND THE STUPID SLOW INTERNET AT MY DORMS SURE AREN'T HELPING THE CAUSE.

HEY... WHAT'VE YOU GOT THERE?

EWW... RAT SLOBBER. THIS NIGHT JUST GETS BETTER AND BETTER.

SKKKSSS

WHERE THE HECK DID THAT DARN RAT GET THIS?

WHAT IN THE WORLD...?

CONFIDENTIAL—PROPRIETARY

TERRAPIN/HUMAN EXO-ARMOR
SYNTHESIS

MILITARY APPLICA—
& BATTLEFIELD A—

HUH?

GEEZ, APRIL... RATS, MYSTERY DISKS, AND NOW YOU'RE SEEING THINGS. WHAT'S...

...NEXT?

STAY BACK!

HELP ME! IN HERE!

UNNG...

VANISH!

WHO THE HELL'S THAT...

...YELLING?

NO ONE ELSE HERE...

HE... ALMOST... KILLED ME.

SPLINTER?

OH... GUH... GUH... GOD...

GAH!

PRESENT DAY.

I MEAN—DO YOU REALLY BELIEVE IT'S POSSIBLE WE'LL FIND RAPHAEL?

IF I DID NOT BELIEVE IT WAS POSSIBLE, LEONARDO, OUR SEARCH FOR YOUR BROTHER WOULD HAVE ALREADY CONCLUDED. *YOU* MUST BELIEVE IT AS WELL.

I... I GUESS I DO, MASTER.

I DON'T KNOW. THE ODDS AGAINST LOCATING A MISSING INDIVIDUAL IN A METROPOLIS THE SIZE OF NEW YORK ARE JUST ABOUT ASTRONOMICAL, IF YOU ASK ME.

BE THAT AS IT MAY, DONATELLO, THERE ARE FAR GREATER POWERS AT WORK IN THIS WORLD THAN MERE STATISTICAL ANALYSIS, AND THEY ARE OFTEN TOO EASILY IGNORED AND UNDERESTIMATED.

WELL, I WISH THOSE POWERS WOULD HURRY UP AND HELP US. I'D RATHER DUKE IT OUT WITH OLD HOB AND HIS GOONS ANY DAY OF THE WEEK THAN WASTE TIME LOOKIN' THROUGH EVERY REEKIN' ALLEY AND PIGEON-POOPED ROOFTOP FOR RAPHAEL.

SO, THEN, MICHELANGELO, YOU CLAIM THE SEARCH FOR YOUR LOST BROTHER TO BE A POOR USE OF YOUR TIME?

NO, MASTER, IT'S NOT THAT. I MEAN, I REALLY DO WANNA FIND RAPHAEL—WE ALL DO. IT'S JUST, WELL...

...IT'S JUST THAT WE'VE BEEN LOOKIN' EVERYWHERE FOR HIM FOR LIKE A YEAR NOW. AND WE'VE GOT ZILCH TO SHOW FOR IT. MAYBE DONNIE'S RIGHT—MAYBE IT IS IMPOSSIBLE.

MAYBE... MAYBE KNOCKIN' HEADS WITH GEEKS LIKE OLD HOB IS WHAT WE SHOULD BE DOIN' INSTEAD—SOMETHIN' THAT MATTERS, YOU KNOW?

I UNDERSTAND YOUR FRUSTRATION, MY SON, AS WELL AS YOUR RESTLESSNESS. I, TOO, AM DISAPPOINTED EACH TIME WE FAIL TO LOCATE YOUR BROTHER.

BUT... I DO NOT BELIEVE WE HAVE LOOKED EVERYWHERE, AS YOU SAY, AND FOR THIS REASON, AND MANY OTHERS, WE MUST CONTINUE OUR SEARCH.

OUR BATTLE AGAINST OLD HOB'S GANG TONIGHT WAS—AS ARE ALL BATTLES WE WILL FIGHT—AN UNFORTUNATE NECESSITY. ANY VALUE DERIVED FROM IT IS HOLLOW AT BEST. OUR WAR HAS ONLY JUST BEGUN, AND HOB IS ONLY THE FIRST OF MANY ENEMIES I FEAR WE WILL BE FORCED TO CONFRONT.

THE ONLY VICTORY WE MUST ACTIVELY PURSUE IS THE RETURN OF RAPHAEL TO OUR CLAN—TO OUR FAMILY. ONLY THEN CAN WE ALLOW OURSELVES A MOMENT OF TRIUMPH, FOR THEN OUR CIRCLE WILL AT LAST BE COMPLETE AND WE WILL BE TRULY READY TO FACE THE HARDSHIPS THAT LIE AHEAD.

UNTIL THEN, HOWEVER, WE MUST CONTINUE TO SEARCH FOR YOUR BROTHER, FOR WITHOUT HIM...

"...WE, TOO, ARE LOST."

SO, YOU'RE HOMELESS AND CAN'T REMEMBER YOUR NAME, HUH? MAN, THAT MUST SUCK. NOT THAT IT'S MUCH BETTER HERE.

YEAH, IT'S TOUGH, I GUESS. BUT IT'S ALWAYS BEEN THAT WAY FOR ME, FAR AS I REMEMBER, SO I'M KINDA USED TO IT.

WELL, I'M CASEY. CASEY JONES. NICE TO MEET YA.

UM... YEAH. THE SAME.

DON'T LEAVE ME HANGING, BRO!

RIGHT. YEAH.

BUMP

HEY, CAN I ASK YOU SOMETHIN', UH, CASEY?

YEAH. SHOOT.

WHAT THE HELL WAS THIS ALL ABOUT TONIGHT? THE THING WITH YOUR DAD AND YOU, I MEAN.

AW, SAME OL' SAME OL'—MY DAD'S A PROFESSIONAL DRUNK, AND NOT THE FUN KIND, YOU KNOW. HE GETS MEAN WHEN HE'S BEEN DRINKIN' SO HE'S PRETTY MUCH MEAN ALL THE DAMN TIME.

BEEN THAT WAY EVER SINCE MY MOM DIED.

THAT SUCKS. I PROBABLY MADE IT WORSE BY BEATING HIM UP, HUH?

NAH, MAN, AIN'T NO BIGGIE. HE PROBABLY WENT TO GET MORE BOOZE WHEN HE TORE OUTTA HERE. THAT LUSH WON'T EVEN REMEMBER ANY OF THIS TOMORROW.

AND, UH... THANKS FOR JUMPIN' IN LIKE THAT, MAN. SOMETIMES HE GETS PRETTY ROUGH, AND I THINK TONIGHT WAS GONNA BE ONE OF THOSE TIMES.

IT'S COOL... NO WORRIES. I'M JUST SURPRISED, IS ALL.

SURPRISED? 'BOUT WHAT?

YOU.

ME?

YEAH, YOU. WHY AIN'T YOU SCARED OF ME? YOU KNOW-OF THE WAY I... I LOOK? EVERYONE USUALLY IS.

HA! YEAH, YOU AIN'T EXACTLY BRAD PITT, ARE YA?

BUT, DUDE, YOU MET MY OLD MAN. NEXT TO HIM, YOU'RE A FRIGGIN' TEDDY BEAR.

THANKS. I GUESS.

DON'T MENTION IT.

YOU HUNGRY, BRO? 'CAUSE I'M STARVIN'!

YEAH, AS LONG AS IT AIN'T GARBAGE. I'M SICK OF EATIN' GARBAGE.

SORRY, DUDE, FRIDGE IS EMPTY.

TELL YOU WHAT—LET ME GET SOME STUFF FROM MY ROOM AND WE CAN GO OUT AND SNAG SOME GRUB.

AND MAYBE...

...WE CAN HAVE OURSELVES SOME FUN ON THE WAY.

I SMACKED THAT GUY UP PRETTY GOOD HUH? DUDE HAD A HARD HEAD, THAT'S FOR SURE.

YEAH, YOU DID, CASEY.

BUT, I'M WONDERIN'—IF IT WAS SO EASY TO BEAT THAT GUY UP WHY DIDN'T YOU FIGHT BACK AGAINST YOUR DAD EARLIER? DRUNK AS HE WAS, I BET YOU COULDA TOOK 'IM.

YEAH, THAT.

MY MOM... SHE DIED LIKE A YEAR AND A HALF AGO FROM CANCER. SHE WAS REALLY SICK FOR A LONG TIME BEFORE SHE WENT AND THAT'S WHAT PUSHED THE OLD MAN OVER THE EDGE. DUDE COULDN'T HANDLE IT, SO I PRETTY MUCH TOOK CARE OF HER WHILE HE DRANK HIMSELF STUPID.

THING IS, MY MOM STILL LOVED HIM A LOT. DON'T ASK ME WHY, BUT SHE DID. AND JUST BEFORE SHE DIED, SHE MADE ME PROMISE TO TAKE CARE OF HIM WHEN SHE WAS GONE— AND TO NOT FIGHT WITH HIM.

I BEEN KEEPIN' MY PROMISE— AT LEAST THE NOT-FIGHTIN'-WITH-HIM PART. I FIGURE THERE AIN'T NO TAKIN' CARE OF THAT BOOZEHOUND ANYMORE, SO I JUST AVOID HIM AS MUCH AS I CAN.

MAN, THAT'S TOUGH.

WELL, WHAT ABOUT YOU? DON'T EVEN KNOW YOUR OWN NAME—NOW *THAT* SUCKS. YOU THINK YOU GOT KNOCKED IN THE HEAD, MAYBE? AMNESIA, OR SOMETHIN'?

MAYBE. I DUNNO. I REMEMBER WAKIN' UP IN AN ALLEY ONE DAY. BUT, BEFORE THAT...?

NOTHIN'.

"...WE GOTTA TELL HOB 'BOUT THIS."

HYAH!

WHOULF!

HA!

UFF!

AGAIN!

SHOW ME AGAIN, DONATELLO. AND THIS TIME, DO NOT LOSE FOCUS OF WHAT IS TRULY IMPORTANT.

INCAPACITATING LEONARDO IS WORTHLESS IF MICHELANGELO IS ABLE TO DO THE SAME TO YOU. YOU MUST STRIKE AND FORGET. THE PAST IS GONE AND ALL THAT MATTERS IS YOUR NEXT MOVE...

...TO CELEBRATE VICTORY PREMATURELY IS TO INVITE EARLY DEFEAT.

YES, SENSEI. I'M SORRY.

APOLOGIES ARE UNNECESSARY, MY SON. I ONLY ASK THAT YOU LEARN FROM YOUR MISTAKES AND STRIVE TO RECTIFY THAT WHICH IS WRONG. TRAINING IS EVERYTHING.

IF WE UNDERESTIMATE THE IMPORTANCE OF TRAINING, THEN WE UNDERESTIMATE THE FORMIDABILITY OF OUR ENEMIES.

UH, MASTER, SPEAKING OF ENEMIES, WHAT EXACTLY IS OLD HOB'S DEAL? I MEAN, WHY'S HE SO HOT TO GET AT US?

WHAT'D WE EVER DO TO HIM?

YES... OLD HOB.

YOU NEED NOT CONCERN YOURSELF WITH SUCH THINGS, MICHELANGELO—AS I SAID, YOU MUST FOCUS ON WHAT *IS*, NOT WHAT *WAS*.

IT IS SIMPLY ENOUGH FOR YOU TO UNDERSTAND...

ERK!

NRAARR?

YROOWW!

DAMN!

KUUSH

PRESENT DAY.

ALL CLEAR, GUYS...

...LET'S GO.

DUDES, I CAN'T BELIEVE WE'RE DOIN' THIS AGAIN.

GIVE IT A REST, MIKEY. YOU KNOW MASTER SPLINTER SAYS FINDING RAPHAEL IS OUR MAIN PRIORITY RIGHT NOW, SO QUIT WHINING.

I'M NOT WHININ', LEO... I'M JUST SAYIN'.

WELL, QUIT SAYING THEN. IT'S GETTING OLD.

I DON'T KNOW, LEO... I'M WITH MIKEY ON THIS.

IF ANYTHING'S GETTING OLD, IT'S CHASING OUR TAILS EVERY NIGHT LOOKING FOR A BROTHER WE'RE NOT EVEN SURE EXISTS.

SO, THAT'S IT? WE CAN PROTECT OTHERS BUT NOT OURSELVES?! C'MON, LEO, DO YOU REALIZE HOW IMBECILIC THAT SOUNDS?

WE *WERE* PROTECTING OURSELVES. BESIDES, I DON'T CARE HOW IT SOUNDS, DONATELLO! IT'S WHAT MASTER WANTS, SO THAT'S ENOUGH!

IS IT, LEO? IS IT REALLY ENOUGH?

LOOK, MIKEY AND I LOVE AND RESPECT FATHER JUST AS MUCH AS YOU DO. IT'S JUST...

...IT'S JUST THAT WE THINK THIS WHOLE RAPHAEL THING— MAYBE IT'S JUST A GUILTY OBSESSION HE HAS, YOU KNOW? LIKE HE COULDN'T SAVE ALL FOUR OF US AND HE JUST DOESN'T WANT TO ACCEPT IT.

MAYBE IT'S TIME WE ALL ACCEPT THAT RAPHAEL WAS PROBABLY KILLED.

DON'T EVEN *SAY* THAT.

WHY? BECAUSE YOU DON'T WANT TO HEAR IT, OR BECAUSE YOU DON'T HAVE THE GUTS TO SAY IT YOURSELF?

I'LL SHOW YOU GUTS, YOU LITTLE—!

WHOA, *WHOA!* THIS AIN'T THE WAY TO DO THIS, BROS. BACK OFF, *BOTH OF YOU!*

MIKEY'S RIGHT, LEO. I'M SORRY.

BUT WHAT I SAID STILL STANDS. EVERY TIME WE DON'T FIND RAPHAEL, WE ACCOMPLISH NOTHING.

MAYBE IT'S TIME WE CHANGE THAT—MAYBE IT'S TIME WE FINALLY GET A LITTLE MORE PROACTIVE ON OUR PATROLS.

BESIDES, IT DOESN'T MEAN WE WON'T BE LOOKING FOR RAPHAEL. WE'LL JUST BE... ENHANCING OUR SEARCHES A BIT. CHANGING THINGS UP.

I... I GUESS IT WOULDN'T HURT, BUT—

THAT'S THE SPIRIT, BRO! LET'S GO KICK SOME ASS, TAKE NAMES, *AND* FIND RAPHAEL! WIN-WIN!

AND, IT'S NOT LIKE MASTER SPLINTER HASN'T TAUGHT US TO ADJUST OUR STRATEGY, RIGHT? YOU KNOW WHAT HE ALWAYS SAYS, LEO...

...CHANGE IS THE ONLY CONSTANT.

HERE YOU GO.

THANKS.

YOU'RE GONNA LOVE THESE, BRO. MADE FROM THE SICKEST MYSTERY MEAT IN ALL OF NYC.

WORKS FOR ME.

DID WE LOSE THE COPS?!

HUH?

YOU KNOW, THERE'S ONLY ONE THING BETTER THAN THEM HOTDOGS...

UF!

JUST SHUT UP AND KEEP RUNNIN'!

OUTTA THE WAY, LOSERS!

...AND THAT'S KNOCKIN' THE CRUD OUTTA TWO-BIT CROOKS.

C'MON!

FIFTEEN MONTHS EARLIER.

THIS IS NOT GOOD, MR. ALLEN. NOT GOOD *AT ALL*.

Y-YES, DOCTOR STOCKMAN, I... I KNOW, SIR.

WELL, THEN, DO YOU ALSO KNOW THE EXTENT OF THE DAMAGES—OF THE LOSSES WE SUFFERED? BECAUSE, IF YOU DO, I'D SINCERELY LIKE YOU TO SHARE THAT PARTICULAR BIT OF INFORMATION WITH ME SOMETIME TONIGHT.

THAT IS, IF YOU DON'T MIND?

UM, YES, DOCTOR... UM, I M-MEAN, NO, SIR... I DON'T MIND.

WELL? I'M WAITING.

UM... OKAY, WELL, THE TERRAPIN EXO-ARMOR SAMPLES ARE INTACT FOR THE M-MOST PART, BUT THE PSYCHOTROPIC S-SERUM WAS A COMPLETE LOSS, AS WAS SPLINTER.

SPLINTER?

Y-YES... SPLINTER WAS THE, UM... RAT WE WERE USING TO T-TEST THE SERUM. WE LOST THE TURTLE SPECIMENS, TOO.

I SEE— QUITE THE TRAGEDY, THAT.

REMIND ME TO HAVE MY SECRETARY ALLOCATE THE FUNDS NECESSARY TO REPLACE THESE POOR LOST CREATURES. I'M GUESSING TWENTY DOLLARS AND A TRIP TO THE PET STORE SHOULD SUFFICE.

THE *MUTAGEN*, MR. ALLEN! NEVER MIND THIS INANE TALK OF MISSING *RODENTS* AND *REPTILES*! TELL ME WHAT HAPPENED TO THE BLOODY *SUPER SOLDIER MUTAGEN*!

Y-YES, SIR, DOCTOR... S-SORRY, SIR.

WE'VE ONLY BEEN ABLE TO, UM, SALVAGE S-SMALL AMOUNTS OF THE MUTAGEN FROM THE ALLEY SO FAR.

BUT, WITH EXTENDED EXPOSURE TO OXYGEN, AND WITH ALL THE DIFFERENT FORMULAE BEING MIXED TOGETHER, IT'S MOST LIKELY T-TAINTED BEYOND, UM... REPAIR.

DAMN IT ALL.

LOSING THE PSYCHOTROPIC SERUM IS BAD ENOUGH NEWS, CONSIDERING WE'LL HAVE TO START FROM SCRATCH IN ITS DEVELOPMENT. BUT THE MUTAGEN?

THE BASIC COMPONENTS FOR THAT WERE SUPPLIED TO US BY *GENERAL KRANG*, AND AT GREAT PERSONAL RISK IF OUR CLIENT IS TO BE BELIEVED. NOW I'M FORCED TO INFORM HIM WE REQUIRE EVEN *MORE*?!

DO YOU REALIZE HOW INFURIATED THE GENERAL WILL BE WHEN HE LEARNS OF THIS DISASTER? ESPECIALLY IF IT'S TRUE THAT *NINJA SOLDIERS* WERE BEHIND THE BREAK-IN. WHAT IF IT TURNS OUT HIS *COMPETITOR* HAS GOTTEN HIS HANDS ON THE MISSING SAMPLES?

THIS COULD *RUIN* ME.

I UNDERSTAND, DOCTOR. BUT, UM... TH-THERE MAY BE A WAY TO GET THE PSYCHOTROPIC COMPOUND BACK WITHOUT HAVING TO START OVER.

HOW?

WELL, IF WE'RE ABLE TO, UM, RECAPTURE SPLIN—ER, THE TEST RAT, WE SHOULD BE ABLE TO EXTRACT W-WORKABLE SAMPLES FROM HIS... UM, *ITS* BLOOD.

HA! REALLY, MR. ALLEN? AND PRAY TELL HOW, IN A MASSIVE CITY INFESTED WITH MILLIONS UPON MILLIONS OF RATS, DO YOU PROPOSE WE FIND THIS "SPLINTER" OF YOURS?

I CAN HELP WITH THAT.

I JUST WANNA KNOW ONE THING—

—DOES THAT FILTHY RAT GOTTA BE *ALIVE* WHEN I BRING HIM TO YOU?

"...SPLINTER'S A *LAB RAT*."

QUICKLY, MY SONS! WE MUST NOT STOP UNTIL WE HAVE PUT A SAFE DISTANCE BETWEEN THE LABORATORY AND OURSELVES.

SAFE?

YES, MY SON, *SAFE*. FATE AND DESTINY HAVE PROVIDED FOR OUR REUNION, AND WE WILL NOT FORFEIT THAT GIFT BY ALLOWING OURSELVES TO BE EASILY CAPTURED.

WE WILL VANISH INTO THE SHADOWS, AS HAS ALWAYS BEEN OUR WAY.

OUR WAY?

I UNDERSTAND THERE IS MUCH YOU DO NOT RECALL, ALL OF YOU. IN TIME YOU WILL REMEMBER, BUT FOR NOW I ONLY ASK FOR YOUR TRUST AND OBEDIENCE AS WE ESCAPE TO OUR NEW LIFE TOGETHER.

AND WITH A NEW LIFE, WE WILL TAKE NEW NAMES... ONES NOW FAMILIAR TO US ALL—

LEONARDO.

DONATELLO.

MICHELANGELO.

AND I AM *SPLINTER*—AS BEFORE, YOUR SENSEI AND FATHER.

THERE IS MUCH WE MUST DO, MY SONS. WE HAVE LITTLE TIME AND THERE ARE MANY THINGS I MUST TEACH YOU—MANY THINGS FOR YOU TO LEARN ONCE AGAIN.

WE WILL FIND A NEW HOME, AND THEN WE WILL FIND YOUR BROTHER...

OFFA ME!

WHO...?

DO YOU THINK IT'S HIM?!

RAPHAEL? IT'S GOT TO BE, DONNIE!

I TOLD YOU, LEO! THIS WAS GONNA BE WIN...

...WIN!

NO.

NO!

URF!

DUDES, LOOK! HOB'S PUNKIN' OUT ON RAPHAEL!

NO, WAIT...

HOB'S GONNA KILL HIM!

"...NO WAY HOB'S TAKING OUT *OUR* BROTHER THAT EASY!"

DON'T FOOL YOURSELF, FREAK. YOU THINK THESE OTHER PUKE-GREEN IDIOTS GIVE A DAMN ABOUT YOU? HA! THEM AND THAT GRIMY RAT LEFT YOU TO DIE ONCE BEFORE—THEY'LL DO IT AGAIN, YOU'LL SEE.

YOU AIN'T NOTHIN' BUT A LAB EXPERIMENT THAT GOT AWAY. HELL, YOU AIN'T EVEN WORTH THE NEEDLE THEY'RE GONNA USE TO SUCK THE BLOOD OUTTA ALL YOU FREAKS—INCLUDIN' THAT DAMN RAT—SOON AS I DRAG YOUR CARCASSES BACK TO *STOCKGEN*.

THOSE EGGHEADS GOT BIG PLANS FOR YOU, YEAH, BUT NONE THAT NEED YOU ALIVE. YOU'RE BETTER OFF DEAD, SEE? *DEAD AND GONE.*

SHUT UP!

NO MORE!

KRAK

I WANT YOU *DEAD!*

DO YOU *HEAR* ME?!

D—!

NO, RAPHAEL...

...NOT LIKE THAT. HE'S BEATEN. LET IT GO, MAN.

BUT, LEO, HOB'S JUST GONNA DO THIS AGAIN. WE—

WE GOTTA BOLT, ANYWAYS—COPS ARE COMIN'!

NO, DONNIE, WE'VE ALREADY DISOBEYED FATHER ENOUGH TONIGHT.

BUT—

I SAID, NO.

EVENTUALLY, THE TEMPEST SUBSIDES.

SENSEI, WE'RE BACK. AND WE'VE BROUGHT SOMEONE WITH US.

AND WHAT BEGAN WITH A FEROCIOUS ROAR...

RAPHAEL.

...ENDS IN UNCERTAIN SILENCE.

WELCOME HOME.

IT IS SIMPLY THE CALM BEFORE THE NEXT STORM...

NOW, MY SONS, THE CIRCLE IS COMPLETE. AT LAST, WE CAN TRULY BEGIN.

THE END

ART BY DAN DUNCAN · COLORS BY RONDA PATTISON

THIS PAGE: ART BY DAN DUNCAN · COLORS BY RONDA PATTISON

OPPOSITE PAGE: ART BY WALTER SIMONSON · COLORS BY RONDA PATTISON

OPPOSITE AND THIS PAGE: ART BY KEVIN EASTMAN · COLORS BY RONDA PATTISON

OPPOSITE AND THIS PAGE: ART BY KEVIN EASTMAN

ART BY **SAM KIETH**